Reflection's

IN TIME

MEMORIES OF LOVE & PAIN

DEMETRIUS IRICK

ACKNOWLEDGMENTS

To the many individuals who have been a blessing in my life, thank you for all of your continued prayers and inspirations throughout the years.

A special thank you to my daughters who continue to be my motivation to reflect on my life and make changes to be a better version of myself. Thank you, ladies, for being such awesome women/girls and putting up with your father as he grows. Although the story hasn't been what I wished for, I am truly blessed and thankful to have shared space, time, and laughter with you.

To the women with who I've loved and shared such awesome memories, thank you for the experience. As life evolves, it was destined that we would create memories together that will last a lifetime, and I am truly saddened that the process of my growth and development caused any of your pain. It is my prayer that peace & happiness find your hearts forever.

To the reader, thank you for taking the time to share these memories. It's my hope that you are able to find something you can relate to and can reflect on the lessons that the experience taught you and shaped whom you have become today. It's through the most painful lessons that we make the greatest advancements in our lives. Give love freely, as each joy and pain are stepping stones to a place of destiny Our Creator is so beautifully placed in your path. Live, Love, and Happiness!

"Your success comes after your next failure."

- Demetrius Irick

"Try harder NOT to leave your dreams & talents in the GRAVE!"

- Demetrius Irick

CONTENTS

INTRODUCTION

This body of work is a compilation of random thoughts, feelings, and emotions I have encountered over the past twenty years and collected in different journals, notebooks, and scrap papers. At first, these were never to be published but only a way to escape my own situations, whether mental or physical.

Finally, I decided to give this body of work to the world uncut. The release of these words is designed for those who struggle with their identity of self. It's for those who feel they are not living up to their total strengths, values, and dreams. It's a journey of emotional instability, poor decisions, and pain both given and received to and from the ones we love the most. It's the feeling of uncertainty and its paralyzing effects on our actions to do and live better. I've spoken to many people throughout my life and have found that every one of them can relate to these feelings at some level.

I hope you enjoy the journey and process of self-love and self-healing.

It's my desire that these words inspire hope and give confirmation to others that it's perfectly fine to be a mixture of love, hate, anger, compassion, a scholar, or an idiot at times in our life's journey. We as humans experience days that we make decisions that are so profound that they can change lives, and on the other spectrum, we can make choices that destroy our progress and hurt those around us.

Let's face it, we as humans are flawed. We have the huge superpower of being a complex mixture of this universe, filled with mysteries, love, catastrophe, and optimism.

We have this unique ability to love an animal and hate another human being. We have this ability to give help to starving children around the world yet walk right by a homeless man begging for his next meal. We have the ability to evolve our way of thinking to see progress in race relations, yet still, people of color are being killed daily due to their race and the historical prejudice our society perpetuates. Women are still battling the glass ceiling and even challenging the right to have dominion over their own bodies. People are still concern about whom someone sleeps with and if sexual orientation is acceptable. We have work to do, but it truly starts with the introspection of self.

I wrote this in all of its imperfections as a reminder that we all are flawed in our own particular way. It is those imperfections that make us human. Remember, you are a child of the Highest, and you are valuable. Live your life to the fullest and dare to dream and execute those dreams.

A FATHER'S LESSON

Actions speak louder than words…I felt I provided love, a house, the latest gadgets, and all kinds of stuff…

Are you telling me it wasn't enough?

-Dad, it wasn't the things that you did or bought…if you listen

It's the things you didn't do…that I was missing…

As I grew…I needed you…to share your pain and your tears…

I needed to know a MAN was human, shed tears, and had their own fears

I didn't need you to be the Terminator or some type of gangsta…that hid his feelings.

I needed you to tell me, show me you were real….

I needed your confirmation that we all must heal.

I needed you to tell me its okay to make a mistake, poor decisions, and choices…

to calm down and listen to your inner being and hold your horses…

Sit with your intuition and trust your gut…

Not, to allow anyone to drag you down and place you in a mental rut.

I needed a shoulder to lean on when I was indecisive, misunderstood, and struggled to maintain.

I needed your hug and strength to tell me I wasn't insane.

-Dad, it wasn't the things that you did or bought…if you listen

It's the things you didn't do…that I was missing…

As I grew…I needed you…to share your pain and your tears…

I needed to know a MAN was human, shed tears, and had their own fears

I'm surrounded by males that lie to me and themselves because that is what society has taught them; Being hard is a man and emotional is Female;

Through this craziness, now women are doing the same;

The reality is they are being taught to be inhumane! How insane!

Taking me and my sister's love in vain…

I see every man through this void, hole, and pain…

The pain of our disconnect Dad and lack of communication;

I am finally being honest with you Dad this is my confession;

The pain has driven me to disconnect from my emotions and act like men

…I find myself …Causing pain to others when will this cycle end?

Dad, I love you and I want us to be better…

I want to start fresh…

I refuse to live this life accepting less…

-Dad, it wasn't the things that you did or bought…if you listen

It's the things you didn't do…that I was missing…

As I grew…I needed you…to share your pain and your tears…

I needed to know a MAN was human, shed tears, and had their own fears

Dear Child, My Angel, I've learned so much from you...I swear we as men walk around with blinders on...truly we don't have a clue...

We try to do the best that we can...with the little we have but...

Bringing a life into this world requires more than I had...I know it's sad.

I should have acquired better resources and understanding to be better and do better...

I see this truth today!

I've learned that I needed to heal the broken child that lived inside of me...I am sorry is really what I want to Say!

I have committed myself to a life of the knowledge of self...

Healing and respect for others...learning to love others and me

-Dad, it wasn't the things that you did or bought...if you listen

It's the things you didn't do…that I was missing…

As I grew…I needed you…to share your pain and your tears…

I needed to know a MAN was human, shed tears, and had their own fears

I see the flaws I possess that stunted my growth…in being the Father & Man you deserved …I'm a changed man I give you my Oath.

I'm sorry and I ask for your forgiveness

I don't expect things to change overnight…but I want you to know that you were entirely right…

There are too many things I've done wrong

But, I refuse to sing a sad song!

Today marks a day of change, a promise that things will not be the same!

No more words, prayers, tears to get a reaction!

Just the stable, consistent views of my actions…

You will see them…up close and afar!

You will know it's because of you that I'd change into a better version

It's because of you I desire to be a better person

-Dad, it wasn't the things that you did or bought...if you listen

It's the things you didn't do...that I was missing...

As I grew...I needed you...to share your pain and your tears...

I needed to know a MAN was human, shed tears, and had their own fears

I Love you, baby...with all my heart

Your words have taught me to give you my heart

To give you and show you through my actions, that my love is not about a transaction.

It's about being genuine, open, and honest; about sharing my inner being and the essence of my beings

It's these actions that give our love meaning

I will tell you, show you and be a living example

Of a Father's Love---

I was told that if I provided shelter and gave you the superficial things you wanted;

I was being a man; I see that wasn't the case

It takes more than things we must share with our ladies

Integrity, honesty, morals are just a taste;

Being present in the moment physically, mentally, and emotionally for our babies;

Sacrificing everything, being a living example of God's Grace

It's a necessity we as men take our rightful place

It's more than money…as you can see;

It's truly about healing and being comfortable being me;

Being comfortable letting people inside;

Putting aside our ego and pride

I love you, Baby, I will do whatever it takes

To be the best version of myself for mine and your sake! Thank you for the lesson I will tell others and show them how to win

How to avoid another generation of lost men

I will no longer sit on the bleacher, and watch the action

I am in the game, gain traction

Thank you my love for your words, love they reached my heart and stirred a much needed change

I know my life will never be the same

Thanks to you and God I'm a new creature…

You are and will forever be my Best Teacher!

ROSES FOR YOU

A red rose is for the richness of past love and memories that will last forever. It represents a life full of passion that was shared for one another. This rose reminds me of a simple kiss and the skill we shared finding each other's tongues. We kissed to find the essence of each other's being... Ahh, the things we learn from a kiss. The passion shared from the sheer discovery of someone new, can it last forever?

A pink rose symbolizes how fragile love can be and the challenges that forced us to question our future together. This rose signifies the hope of a future that will be filled with respect, love, and compassion for each other. This pink rose teaches me to have humility, respect, and to never take love for granted.

A yellow rose symbolizes rebirth, renewal, or recommitment regardless of the faults we each possess. We must find salvation in the strength of each other and work towards building a better life together. This yellow rose reminds me that relationships are a process of consistent trials and issues, some small, others grander. We should always set our attention and focus on building a solid ground or foundation for our love.

Roses of every color bring about a rainbow of emotions, energies, memories, scents, and can be found to bring tremendous smiles. When you think of a rose, what memory comes to mind? What do you remember about the smell? Where did this rose take you in your mind?

MY GREATEST FEAR

Sometimes, I ask the question, "Where would I be without you?" I reflect on days of old, stealing a glance of your silhouette as you showered; I glared at your splendor and felt the affection we once shared rush through my veins. I remember you laying on top of my chest at night as you rest your head at peace. I remember the smell of your pillow, your perfume in the room as you left for work. It lingered in the room.

I push the thought to the back of my mind, hating to even imagine life without you. My greatest fear is a life without you; I forced myself to confront these fears and saw only pain, darkness, and sadness. I saw your cries, felt your pain, and blamed myself for each teardrop, each doubt or question that haunts your nightmares. The pain in my chest and tears I shed haunt me to this day.

I should have loved you better; I know that today. There are a million things I could have done differently to get a better outcome. A decision to not do anything is a decision to keep things the same. Wow, even in my inaction, I committed to the demise of our relationship. Life and the lessons we learn from our decisions help to shape us into our current state of growth. The pain has sharpened a lot of my intuition and understanding of my feelings, emotional delinquency, and growth opportunity.

I understand that I can't wish for a better past; therefore, I do the work of understanding myself better today. I do the hard work of learning to understand my destructive patterns, thought processes, and behavior. The work consists of dealing with negative self-talk and destructive childhood patterns. I understand

Today that even in my physical maturity in the body, emotionally, and in some cases, mentally I was still a child. I admit today that mentally, in some respects, I thought like a child. The pain we caused each other has been such a burden and one that is a daily reminder of decisions and consequences. This relationship has been the hardest thing I've endured, yet I smile at the memories that have helped shaped the man I have become.

As the days continue, I grow a little stronger, equipped with an unforeseeable strength to face the uncertainty life has for me. I have to relinquish my fears and trust that our God has a plan that I just don't understand, and that's not easy. I embrace the uncertainty with hope. I embrace the uncertainty with the optimism that, wherever I land, my Creator has my back, and until I close my eyes… HIS plan will always be for my greater good.

I believe my steps are protected and coordinated by THE ONE! As I journey, I know that I will keep you near, in my mind and heart. I will forever have our memories to hold onto. The love we shared will forever live in my heart and mind. Although my greatest fear is losing you, I will stand strong, knowing it was me who did you wrong. Understanding that every action has a reaction, understanding your actions was a reflection of my inaction and poor choices. I understand my role in our destruction and will forever live the motto: ***"Some mistakes you just can't come back from."***

I am thankful for the experiences and the moments we've shared together. I love you… It was such a pleasure spending time with you, sharing love and life. What shall our future hold, it's uncertain, but part of me knows that we shouldn't be together.

PAIN

The pain I caused can never be forgiven; I realize that today. In my selfishness, I only wanted what was best for me and didn't consider the ramifications of my choices. I never examined how it would affect the lives of everyone involved, families or friends. I never considered the void it would cause: holidays, Christmas alone, no Thanksgiving dinner together. Some mistakes you can't come back from...I will never forget this motto. The children and how they would process this disconnect. How will they operate in this new norm? Will it force them closer to one another or will it harden their hearts and search for affection in different places?

It was my belief that I could love you enough for both of us. I believed my love would rub off on you and equip us with a shelter no one could destroy. I was under the misconception you could love me in all of my brokenness and internal turmoil. I was under the illusion that my desire, my wants, could be yours, and that you would one day want me just as much as I wanted you. Foolish, I know ...I know that was only a dream, a fantasy I wanted.

The pain crippled me to my core; yet, I understand its origins. I understand your reasoning for the void and disconnect. I was selfish in many ways, and now I understand that pain I saw in your eyes. I understand today the reason your touch wasn't the same, distant that of a stranger. Your glaze as you looked at me & past me at the same time!

The trauma from your words & actions rendered me voiceless, abused; I have never felt so helpless. The internal pain coupled with the lack of having an outlet to disperse the raw emotions allowed self-destructive patterns to grow.

The distancing of myself from family and loved ones only added to your influence and control.

There are days when I am unable to express myself verbally, emotionally, or rationalize the pain. I dig deep and try to understand my feelings, the pain, the circumstances, and want answers. Why is it so difficult for me to find my voice? Why am I allowing this verbal abuse?

I wish you could understand my feelings, relate to the waves of the internal sea of rage smashing against the shore and rocks. Someday, I wish you could articulate the pain into words that you experienced from our relationship. I wish we could have addressed what we both experienced differently. I hope you can understand I did not desire to cause you pain.

I know to seek revenge is petty and childish, truly immature; yet I wasn't strong enough to walk away from what I thought was love. I felt even in the midst of the crazy cycle, we loved one another, and the acts of injustice we displayed against each other were a way we dealt with our anger, distrust, and flaws. We needed better tools to deal with our anger, disagreements, and frustrations instead of causing pain to the ones we love the most. I relished in that forbidden area of vengeance, which according to the Bible is the Lord's. I sought out vengeance and delighted in its simple pleasure. I allowed it to ruin my inner light and bury the seeds that lived inside.

LONELY RELATIONSHIP

Have you ever been in a relationship and still felt alone? Have you evaluated the relationship and realize you have evolved beyond the current situation? What are your options when this happens? I struggled with staying versions leaving. Should I add another layer by seeking attention elsewhere? Do I have the courage to be authentic in my relationship…to tell my truth…I am not happy anymore! How can we fix this? Is there anything worth savaging? I have this internal battling going on…am I being selfish? Is this relationship healthy for the two of us? Have you ever been in a relationship and still felt alone?

My mistake was I decided to stay and fake it until we make it. I was a coward afraid to stand on my own two feet by myself alone. I realize today it was one of the worst decisions I could have made for my overall mental health. I allowed obligations to keep me still avoiding the much-needed silent time needed to heal. Being alone would mean I had to face my demons by myself. Being alone means I had nothing to distract me. I was weak to your touch, to the smell of your essence. Have you ever been in a relationship and still felt alone?

Have you ever been in a relationship and still felt alone? Was it that your body called me, and I was addicted to its playground. Was it your taste, your lips, your kiss? I wanted only to grow old and pinch your booty when you walked past. I smiled at the thought but know it will never be. I wanted to see your smile even though all the tears in my eyes blinded me. With each tear, I gained even more determination to fight through our brokenness. I fought for the chance to win your heart again the fact that I knew I could never have you completely again. Have you ever been in a relationship and still felt alone?

THE LOVE OF MY LIFE

The love of my life left me just like everyone that ever loved me. The love of my life caused more pain than the loss of my closest relatives. She gave herself to many others leaving her heart out of business for me. You made a fool of me, I realize that my best wasn't good enough today. You chose to break my heart by lying with another and having a child. Unlike most, I decided to stay, but to my dismay, I couldn't forgive or forget the injustice, it stayed in my heart. I wanted you to feel the pain and torment that I endured. It felt like an icepick piercing your skin it's the only example that comes to mind. The circumstances changed the essence of who I was, forcing me into a mental cocoon, creating moments of temporary insanity, literally out of mind choices. The idea of exploring this world without my companion never crossed my mind. I was blinded and let the years grow adding to our isolation. You could rarely do any wrong in my eyes. No one could love you the way I did but I understand today that I wasn't enough.

The love of my life seeks to find attention in others. Your beauty captivates the room it raises the temperature of the room for most men causing instinctual desire and for me unwanted attention. You didn't see "Me" and the man I had continually evolved into. Trapped by the pain, and jailed by the betrayal, your only healing was from the attention of another. I feel it daily in the loss of my family, as the isolation and resentment crept into my heart. The pain pushes my faith to the brink of insanity, yet I'm still here.

The love of my life has gone to be with another, and although I don't deserve to have her, it hurts like hell, the thought of another touching her, making her smile play like a broken record. And yet, part of me desires it, understands it,

And has gotten used to the feelings of emptiness that lingers in my heart. I want her to have happiness, be at peace, and carefree because that's what she deserves. Deep inside of my being, I knew I wasn't able to live up to her demands, love, or desire yet I held on to the fantasy. Then reality hit and I had to be honest with myself she needed something I was unable to provide.

To the love of my life, you will see the positive impact I will leave on this world. Thank you for sharing space, time, and energy in this dimension to create a better version of myself. You will always be the love of my life.

I'M SORRY

Unfortunately, my evolution was too slow.

I wasn't the one you could rely on.

My emotional detachment kept me from speaking my truth;

And pushed us away

A male can be so weak with regard to their feelings.

It was in those times I struggled and I needed healing.

I needed a blessing only our Creator was able to grant,

The kind that would be life-changing and keep me on track.

I'm sorry I brought you into this world of mine without being whole myself.

I'm sorry I didn't seek out professionals to increase my emotional wealth,

I needed a better way to deal with my internal demons and insecurities.

It was through this that I learned maturity,

The maturity needed to love in a manner that gives life,

Avoiding the traps that create strife;

Thank You for the PEACE of mind,

for leaving the past behind.

Peace allowed a resurrection or rebirth of the true essence.

It allowed me to be a blessing.

Thank you, and I'm sorry for the bumps that I put in the road.

I now know it's those bumps that made me whole!

I will always love you.

I FINALLY DECIDED

I finally made the decision to be a man, strong and confident in my decisions, to avoid being double-minded with every thought.

I finally decided to express my affection to all humans, promote positive energy, and live a life filled without negative karma.

I finally decided that being evil or contributing to the destruction of another person is just not the avenue I would like to be remembered for so I changed my friends.

I decided to be a living example of someone who is humbled yet striving to be a person of excellence,

To develop my character and standing in truth,

To avoid backstabbers, lying, and deceitful ways and anything that will destroy me and others.

I finally have a life mission and that is to enhance the lives of those I come in contact with what's yours?

It's time to represent the blessings of life and live one that concentrates on the positive side of life.

I finally decided to LOVE MYSELF!

LOVE IS?

Love is God, and God is Love.

Love is all of the good things from the heaven above;

I reflect on the best times shared and always remember how much you cared;

Since the beginning of time, relationships have gone sour.

It's one of the reasons we must take them hour-by-hour,

To stand in faith and avoid evil thoughts which come to devour.

The bliss, the power of love will always shower.

The sun will shine even after a stormy day,

I worship you and give thanks to all the things you have to say,

Those whispers in my ear, a gentle reminder that you are there

To carry me when needed, to avoid the mental despair.

I will always love you, and this you know.

As I write these words, the emotions start to flow.

I scream, "I love you!

I love you as you can tell by these words,

 I hope they show you this.

I am so thankful for the blessings you have put into me.

I have no reason to be down or uncertain when I face a storm,

If for no other reason but to confirm you will always be there and take me to new heights above all norms.

I am just happy to have the ability to give thanks to you this day.

Thank you, God, for all you have done in the past, present, and future each and every day.

IF ONLY YOU KNEW

If only you knew my love was true.

You don't have to pursue another lover again.

I promise to be with you until the end.

If you don't know by now, you will never know my heart.

Maybe it's my time to let you go.

Is that so?

Our past deeds have drawn us to question our relationship.

I believed we could have conquered anything if we stuck together.

That belief was the cornerstone for my promise forever.

Now, darkness has entered, and I don't think we can weather the storm.

If only you knew, my love was true.

You don't have to pursue another lover again.

I promise to be with you until the end.

If you don't know by now, you will never know my heart.

I'm planning to be here until the end.

I will fight for you until my last breath,

Until there is nothing left;

If you only knew how deep the pain runs and how it's threatening my faith.

If only you knew, my love was true.

If only you knew, you wouldn't have to pursue another lover again.

I've always planned to be there until the end.

I am aware of the love I seek and share; one can't compare to the love of Our God. It's HIS example I will put my trust into,

His example has taught me not to rush into anything unprepared. If you only knew God, you would know HE blessed my heart to love you through it all

MEMORY LANE

Since the summer of 92', I knew your love would be there and true.

All the late-night conversations, I prayed that we had no confrontations;

I wanted nothing to come between the two of us.

But, next came lust.

It took us to a dream world,

And it was then that I knew you would be my girl

I wanted someone I could trust…

You know, a good girl,

A wholesome lover,

Closer than any brother.

I remember having a hundred breakups during those days;

It wasn't easy trying to figure out each other's ways.

Each time, we came back together more determined than the next,

Unified but not knowing what to expect.

It was then I knew you were a sincere girl.

I was gonna give you the world.

It was you for me and me for you,

My eternal dream lover to spend eternity,

Someone to grow old with and share sweet memories,

To put ben-gay on my back and knees.

I know problems will arise,

But it doesn't change that look in your eyes.

Our future has a long journey ahead,

Yet, I am thankful to share this road of life with you

And tackle anything that comes our way.

'Cause our love is true.

HOW MUCH LONGER?

How much longer before we share each other's embrace?

How much longer until it's time to see your face?

O, Heavenly Father provide me with a clue

I'm so distraught I don't know what to do;

How much longer before we share each other's embrace?

How much longer until I see your face?

I believe in you Father, so I pray every day, and night.

I believe in you, Father, to one day see the light,

To share your glory and be with my past loved ones,

To share laughter with old acquaintances before I'm called home

I strive to be a better me for my unborn son

I am ready to hear the words "Your work here is done."

I will let the light shine that you've given me.

I will maneuver the traps and vines in order to see

I will bask in your glory,

And share my story. A story of perseverance, poor choices, cuts and bruises

One that holds no punches and fights to the end

Listening for that inner voice, to quiet my soul with a

Amen

IT'S BEEN TOO LONG

It's been too long since we've shared each other's embrace.

It's been two lifetimes since I've seen your face,

You hid your heart from me for mine was hollow;

I didn't understand how dark my heart was, how shallow,

You tried to fill the void I had by loving me.

I fought tooth & nail against it. I couldn't see.

I understand today your beauty and strength brought me to you.

I knew gaining your love and respect wouldn't be easy to do.

As I learned more about you, it was your heart and compassion that swept me off my feet.

If only you could hear these words before it's too late.

If only the visions I've received were not our fate.

The pain in my chest, tears in my eyes, and I ask and wonder why.

Why were things so broken, love dried, and no way to recover?

Why I lost my friend, my lady, and my lover?

The insight of knowing things will never be the same, and because of what?

Some mind game?

It's been too long since we've shared each other's embrace.

It's been two lifetimes since I've seen your grace.

I see my life unfold, and peace is taken away.

I sit in this lonely room and wipe the tears away.

Many tears at night as I cry and pray,

Pray, "Dear Creator, remove me from this place.

It's lonely, and I don't like the way my mind is running about.

I need to escape. I have to get out.

Give me the faith to do the work without doubt.

Give me the strength to manage to do better.

Give me the discipline to follow your word to the letter.

Dear God, I should have listened to the complaints.

I should have made the changes if I wanted another fate.

Now, a future with you will never be.

I will lie in my bed with many regrets;

I created this outcome due to my neglect.

It's been too long since we've shared each other's embrace.

It's been two lifetimes since I've seen your face.

THE ONLY WOMAN

You have given me the best of you, and made my dreams come true;

You are truly the only woman in this world for me.

After all the things that you have done, by blessing me with girls, it makes it easy to say that you are the only woman for me.

I never thought that love could be so rewarding & kind until you came and gave me joy and peace of mind;

You are truly the only woman in this world for me.

You are my sincere side, truly my better half,

You represent love, patience, and beauty.

In you, I have found why God created women,

To bring forth life, especially black women.

Your essence is a reflection of the depth of your strength,

Your courage, and ability to shine a light on the darkest of situations;

Save a whole generation through your sacrifice

It's easy to see why you are the only woman for me

You have given me the best of you, and you've made my dreams come true.

You are truly the only woman in this world for me.

In you, I have found my children's mother.

In you, I discovered, a lover like no other.

I can't begin to tell you how much you mean to me,

How often I pray and thank God for you.

You are truly the only woman in this world for me, and I love you, forever.

SEX

Sex.

It's not everything but what does it say when we are no longer attracted to each other. What does it mean when our bodies don't respond to each other?

Sex is a healthy part of any good relationship

Then why are we not having this sacred connection?

Are we doing it enough? Are you satisfied with our connection?

Why the mental blocks that I can't get an erection?

What options are available to us to jump-start our relationship? Tantric yoga role-plays

Anything to re-established our connection

Sex.

Amazing, as it is it's not enough alone,

I need mental masturbation, the mental stimulation to pair in union the touch, caressing of our bodies leaves me desiring more. To have someone that has the same desires, aspirations, sexual energy that love to explore,

the aggressiveness, competitiveness in bed is what I desire…

and when I don't have it, the need to have it is dire

I feel unhappy, angry and it makes me desire to be with another

Sex.

It's more than physical, it the mental connection coupled with the organismic experience.

Most women believe men only want sex but it's our way of connection

Why do you trivialize our method of intimacy as being shallow?

It's why we will leave our home in search of another, to uncover this mystic

Experience of connection; it's a feeling that men truly can relate too

It's more than just the physical act, it's our emotion, physical and mental connection;

It's one of the few things that have us operating within all dimensions; Mind, Body, Spirit.

When done with the right person is heavenly

Sex is not everything, yes I agree but it's important for every man that includes me!

INVISIBLE

Invisible, I cry when I'm alone. Embarrassed, by emotions of being inadequate

A failure from keeping my family structure, giving way to life's destructive patterns

Feelings of self-assurance were beaten out of me.

Never have I felt so worthless, incomplete, and foolish. Should I just end it?

Will this be the day I meet my maker?

I feel I don't deserve the grace of seeing another day

I smile every day, although I'm so sad inside.

Why can't anyone hear my cry?

Am I that good at being a pretender?

Of living a life of make-belief and or is

Everyone just worried about his or her life issues to care.

I am invisible and cry when I am alone, embarrassed by my emotional inadequacy.

To express my feelings and stand strong, I ask myself do I deserve to carry on? Is this the day that I meet my maker?

Trapped inside my mind... such a horrible fate.

Contemplating whether this would be my date.

With death, it feels much easier

To drown out the noise and have a place of peace.

I struggle daily to live up to an expectation that always changes.

Cold, sleepless nights like strangers. I ask myself do I deserve to carry on?

Is this the day that I meet my maker?

WHEN WILL YOU

Figure out you are a fucked up individual?

You carry more darkness than light

When you realize you have an internal fight?

When will you realize that you are capable of being calculating, devious, and destructive?

When will you acknowledge the dark energy you possess and learn to work on it?

Learn and apply the Hermetic principles, to establish discipline

They have worked for thousands of years for many men

When will you learn?

When will you realize that you want so much

yet lack the willpower to go out and take it?

Will you ever understand that you want someone

to love you but you don't love yourself?

When will you deal with your self-hatred?

Correct your self-destructive ways and lack of discipline?

When will you cherish your health?

It's the key to your wealth!

When will you cherish the people in your life?

Will you fight for them and forget about yourself?

Will you live and put others before your own needs?

Will you make the sacrifice and believe the Creator's mission for your life.

When will you be a better father, role model, brother, and citizen?

Will you learn to tap into your divine purpose?

Will you ever stop fighting the light inside of you?

When will you...Be what the Creator created you to be?

LAST DAYS

I feel it,

That overwhelming weight engulfing me,

Flashes of memories at a million miles per second.

The thoughts race like a NASCAR driver circling the track.

They run through my mind randomly, seamlessly without direction.

They haunt me with my failures and remind me that I have an opportunity

Each day to work towards inner peace.

The grief is heavy my heart blackened by the pain

What can I do to finish my project,

The assignment that was given by God,

Keep your heart pure, thoughts and actions in alignment

The disappointment for not living up to His standards.

"Tomorrow never comes" are words you should live by.

Make the most of each opportunity to touch someone's life in a positive way.

I've ruined too many lives instead of healing and inspiring.

The journey to right my wrongs and cleanse my heart is needed

To survive the scale of life/ having eternal life without the negative karma

There is nothing more about the gift of life than making the most out of each moment.

Help as many people as possible, try to leave more positive than negative.

To make the best out of your life by using your gift before the time elapse.

In the end, what is it all for? What is this life about? How will the end look for you?

HURT PEOPLE

I never understood the phrase, "Hurt people hurt people."

I never understood why the very people we love are the ones who hurt us the most.

Why do certain things happen to certain people?

I understand today why hurt people hurt people.

Why have I never spoken about my abuse?

I was a broken man who wanted to be whole but didn't know how to.

The ability to speak about the things that hurt us the most can be the breakthrough that unlocks the bondage for another and ourselves.

The desire to withdraw and shut down only prevents me from looking in the mirror. The mirror is scary and requires a true assessment

I understand today why hurt people hurt people.

I poured my shortcomings on the table, and she was forced to deal with my broken pieces.

I took away her ability to choose, and it ruined her and me.

The sense of abandonment felt during my breakdown,

The loneliness, fear of being misunderstood, or forgotten plagued my psyche.

It was this pain that prevented letting my guard down, my true emotions

I understand today why hurt people hurt people.

I pushed people away as a coping skill.

I see this pattern in my life even today.

I traveled with this torment alone when all I had to do was share that burden.

I understand today why hurt people hurt people.

Her lack of emotions was because of our disconnection… my refusal to be authentic about myself… the good, bad, and the ugly.

I was too afraid to lose her to the truth.

I understand today why hurt people hurt people.

It to me a long time to realize she couldn't give me something she didn't have herself.

From the time I was shown my death, I've been running from it,

Trying to do better in this life before I die.

So, now, my mission is to leave this world

a little better than it was when it was given to me.

But, I understand the difficulty this presents when you are hurt and unwilling to heal.

I understand today why hurt people hurt people.

I am proud that I had a chance to see a part of me

that wasn't always shady my daughter.

I wished I was a better example for my children, my wife.

She deserves better than I could ever give.

I understand today why hurt people hurt people.

AM I A GOOD PERSON?

I have always been told to be good.

I believed, at my core, that I was good.

I tried to leave more smiles than frowns when I awake each day,

And to be mindful of the words I say.

I am intentional about not causing much harm.

I'm forced to recognize the warmth from my charm.

"Am I a good person?" is a question I ask at night.

Am I deserving of forgiveness and passage to the light?

I want to be known as a contributor to mankind & the human race,

My time is dwindling right before my face.

It's almost that time for me to say my eternal goodbye.

Will, I hear "Good Job" my faithful son.

Or will I be scolded, eyes fill with tears, as I cry

"Am I a good person?" is a question I ask at night.

Am I deserving of forgiveness and passage to the light?

I have been blessed to be an inspiration to some yet a monster to others.

Hurt people, I loved and offended my brothers.

I've given to charity and helped homeless men

Yet my heart is still dark, mind confused and full of sin

I have shared laughter with many and created tears for others.

Drunk beers with friends and loves, and fucked over other children's mothers.

I have sacrificed for loved ones at the expense of my own happiness.

All for the chance of hearing "Be blessed".

"Am I a good person?" is a question I ask at night.

Am I deserving of forgiveness and passage to the light?

I have said my prayers as I was taught at night.

Yet, there still lies a question about my heart's light

I have given mercy and forgiveness to those who have offended me.

Yet, my sin swims amongst my heart like the sea

But does that make me a good person? or bad?

I am truly interested in the outcome regardless of how sad

I have avoided many temptations but still fell victim to a few.

I have been stuck at a crossroad, not knowing what to do.

I've saved lives and destroyed others,

Abandoned loved ones and lost connections with my brothers.

I've struggled with being a good guy, at times being shy;

I've struggled with letting the demons die.

"Am I a good person?" is a question I ask at night.

Am I deserving of forgiveness and passage to the light?

So, this duality I face, is it just me?

Or are we all faced with these thoughts but afraid to see?

LOST SOUL

Lost souls are produced from the individual being lost in life.

With no strong conviction or clear path, they live life in a constant bubble,

Never push themselves or get misguided ending up in trouble

Lost their focus, on the eternal and lived by the hour

Wasting their precious life until there was nothing left

Walking around aimlessly, in search of the next distraction

Be it drugs, wine, sex, or another of their choice

Never tapping inward to that inner voice

Traveling this dark road, alone but surrounded by many

Until there a fork in the road or dead-end

Wake up dear soul and listen to that inner being

Before you are trapped wondering, lost out in the cold

Trapped in a space and time as a lost soul.

Believe in the unseen as it's real and I know you know this.

There have been too many examples in your life to doubt HIS existence

Your resistance doesn't dim the light that HE has saved you often

Think back…on your actions that should have had you in a coffin

Many years ago, I was given a vision.

I saw death and was afraid and calm.

Nervous from the finality, but a presence kept me calm, a sense of familiarity.

Had I died before? Did I get a do-over? Is this Karma?

Wake up dear soul and listen to that inner being

Before you are trapped wondering, lost out in the cold

Trapped in a space and time as a lost soul.

I recalled shootouts. Was I there?

Flashes of life and death so close to my life, I could smell it

Car wrecks walking away with minor scrapes.

Did I walk away? Chaos lives inside pushes, the barriers to my peace

Until I am asleep I will get to know the relief

Where do those spirits go?

Do they just exist in my mind? Are they eternal and we play life over and over until we get it right?

Wake up dear soul and listen to that inner being

Before you are trapped wondering, lost out in the cold

Trapped in a space and time as a lost soul.

A LETTER OF APOLOGY

I   As a man and leader of the house, I didn't have a vision of where the house should be nor a plan on how to get us there. This lack of foresight led nowhere but bum-fumbling each day. I was ill-equipped, stepping into these shoes, so I did what came naturally, live for today and not tomorrow. The problem this presented was the inability to make provisions that can prepare a family for a stable future past the current day.

I've learned that this is not okay and unacceptable for women, which led to a lack of trust, stability, and led to uncertainty from my wife as to whether I could be the man of the house. Being the woman, she is, she attempted to fill the role, but there are just some things a man should and must do. I believe we all should have our roles in the house, and I wasn't fulfilling my part of the deal.

II.   This is a continuation of the first, as I was horrible at saving and managing money. Yet another example of failure in leadership is that much is given, much is expected. It seemed I never made enough money, but realistically, I made a great living. Yet, it was my management of the money that granted me the luxury of having zilch!

The stress levels of the money slipping through our hands infuriated my wife. I could see the vein in her forehead ready to burst when it was time to pay bills or pay taxes each year. It was depressing for me, seeing our pay stubs and how much money came through our hands.

III.   I really never cared enough about the feelings of anyone other than myself. I was so selfish, wanted what I wanted regardless of what anyone else thought, cared, or felt. I was going to get it. This ideology was driven by the philosophy, "Life is short, so do whatever you want to do and worry about it later."

I never took the time to reflect on what my wife wanted or needed. I never thought that I should, maybe, adopt a new philosophy. I would do the superficial things, yes, but the root of her request of being the leader went unmet. I couldn't hear her, we were not speaking each other's love language to relate.

IV.   I realized I caused my wife severe pain and emotional stress in the infant stages of our marriage. I wasn't empathetic to the way she processed her pain and demanded that she figure out a way to "just get over it" or "deal with it." This insensitive and arrogant way of thinking caused a wall of emotional breakdown that was impossible to remove.

I realized, after years in the relationship, that the emotion of past issues was still very prevalent today in our marriage. I never sought out a counselor for us to deal with and process these devastating tragedies on a consistent basis.

Unfortunately, I allowed it to go unresolved, which assisted in the lack of desire and respect, along with disinterest in ways to actively make the relationship work.

We were both just waiting for something different yet hoping our relationship would get better. We should have sought help after we realized the problems were not going anywhere. But we refused and, instead, allowed space and a wall to stifle our marriage for many years ultimately leading to divorce. I always heard that communication is key in a relationship but I have come to learn that it's the communication coupled with comprehension of each other put into action that is key.

V.   To my daughters that watched in silence and learned the wrong characteristics of a man, I am truly sorry. I didn't realize at the time the difference between being a boy, male, and man. I understand today I was stuck in the male phase of growth. I displayed the physique, made money, and supplied tangible, physical, worldly things…things that really don't even matter. I see the value should have been on my self-development, so I could have taught you the ethics, morals, and values that one should have for another human being. I understand I operated out of deficiency and wasn't strong enough, equipped enough, or whole enough spiritually to lead myself. I operated and welcomed chaos and in return pour out unthinkable pain on your lives. I understand that I gave you guys a horrible example and a low bar for men which has affected you and your relationships to this day. I understand that my lack of having a value system and standing solid on those values, morals, and principles led to you seeing the worst version of myself. I get it today having a better understanding of karma and the importance of having a heart & soul that is pure or at least in Ma'at (balance) it's the most important thing. I am truly sorry I failed you guys. I am doing the work today, the inner work, healing, charting a new path for my life with hopes of one day gaining your trust. I will always love you. Dad

CHOICES

Words can't define the level of mistrust I feel for you.

I've lost my friend and life partner behind poor decisions, what a man to do?

When your choices hurt the hearts of others;

It's difficult to recover; sleeping with another; entertain somebody new;

All in an attempt to renew; a feeling, a spark, or an emotion of any sort;

Produce more pain, sorrow, and disgrace.

Such selfishness shouldn't exist, yet I'm daily reminded of my loss.

There are some mistakes we can't come back from

I'm told with time, all wounds will heal, but it's too fresh to see any kind of future today.

Our decisions and the actions we display; will they always hinder me in this way?

When the feelings of others aren't respected; will love and happiness be neglected?

When the lack of empathy and compassion is reduced…is it possible to be reproduced?

One good decision could impact generations in a positive way, and one bad decision could impact them for a generation and a day. Let's raise our children to make healthy choices, for the future generation to avoid the losses. Let's teach them morals and values; for it's those things that will shape the world for future generations to come.

WHY WE STAY

I was first attracted to your looks but fell in love with your strength

At the time all I wanted was someone to dare, to care

In you, I found my eternal love, my heaven.

As the years past we grew apart, we both was ill-equipped to deal

With affairs of the heart; when days are rainy, and I don't have an umbrella

Our parents never taught us to deal with this. So we result to things and ways we always have; you lash out in verbal abuse, me shutting down when mad

How does such brightness become so dim? Where do you go when your house is filled with dismay? Why should we stay?

Physical beauty wasn't enough to disguise your inner battle.

Abuse comes in many forms; the scars sometimes are not visible.

It's a miracle; we raised healthy children thru the darkness

It's probably because we numbed our pain and became heartless

To deal with our issues we stayed intoxicated, medicated on booze, wine, and mixed drinks; anything to keep us from having to think; about the difficulties of relationships without the tools; hating to be one another's fool

I struggle to understand how someone so beautiful could be so dark

What tainted your heart? How does such brightness become so dim?

Where do you go when your house is filled with dismay?

Why should we stay?

It wasn't your body that made me stay.

It was that you challenged me to live a better way.

Relationships are rough, usually why most don't last.

It's just easier to hit and run to get a piece of ass.

Redefining ourselves through rough times requires some soul searching and honesty

Being open to others points of view & realizing it's not about "ME"

In a relationship, it truly takes two committed souls

If the plan is to truly grow old; together we can do anything if we are on the same accord, and we don't get bored. But if we do decide to call it quits

It's only our fault, maybe it wasn't legit

How does such brightness become so dim?

Where do you go when your house is filled with dismay?

The question still remains why should we stay?

FAILURE

You can never fail if you've never attempted anything.

It's that fear that paralyzes you and keeps you stagnant running still

Fear is a gauge of your true heart's will;

A test of your belief system within

Time and time again, if you don't act, you can never win;

Failure is but an educational lesson

It's a way to recalculate; it's really a blessing

A gauge that points you in the right direction

When in turn you figure out the true lesson

It's about never giving up, moving towards the next clue

as long as you wake up, there is work to do;

Failure is not the destination but a motivation that you're on track

The more you fail the more you realize the Universe has your back;

The lesson sharpens your skills and toughens your resolve

It gives you inspiration when others fall

Those willing to change will be the ones who obtain it.

If you want it, you have to do something differently.

Are you willing to put in the work?

SILENT HEROES

To the Silent Heroes who help shape, mold, and encourage future world leaders.

Africans always knew it took a village to raise a child

It's the influences of the parents and environment that produce the fruit of the future

The family structures are the heroes that dictate the direction of the world

To those who stand for what is right, those that always kept their heart light;

To those that fight; to ensure our world continue to be prosperous; thank you for the ancestors that have left, but placed a special blessing in you before they left;

To the Silent Heroes that fought for their families and invested in their children.

Those individuals that gave up their dreams to instill them in their seeds;

Self-sacrificing their individual needs; those that help to pave the way;

With aspirations of the world being better and seeing a better day;

Be it independence from imperialist rule

Or the escape of physical bondage, rape, slavery, or all things cruel

The true lesson is taught indoors, it's the teaching of living a decent life

Being kinds to others, treating them like you want to be treated; a life without strife;

To the silent heroes who sacrificed day and night,

To those that fight; to ensure our world continue to be prosperous; thank you for the ancestors that have left, but placed a special blessing in you before they left.

HOW DO YOU LOVE?

How do you love when the person you love doesn't love you?

How do you build when the one you love loves another?

How do you love when your heart has been neglected?

How does one recover from an affair of the heart, abuse, or infidelity?

How do you strive when love has been tainted?

How do you create a new canvas to paint?

How do you love when every time I see my lover there's an image of them kissing another?

How do you love when you feel dirty after every kiss?

How do you love when your touch has you trapped in the pain of your inner thoughts?

How do you love when the sounds of passion replays of another?

How do you love I asked my family, my brother?

How do you love when it's in this place, can we recover?

How do you love I ask as I walk this beach feet in the sand?

How do you love in this space, time, this physical land?

How do you love when the person you love doesn't love you?

How do you build when your heart is partially with another?

How do you avoid the pain, knowing things will never be the same?

How do you love when things will never be the same?

How do you get your heart to reopen and flow?

How does the heart know to illuminate and glow?

When will it be free to love and experience joys & pains?

How do you love when the sounds of passion replays of another?

How do you love I asked my family, my brother?

DUE TIME

Dear God, I know you want me to be happy but how do I get there?

How do I get out of this fantasyland of fairytale love and brokenness?

How much longer must I wish for a better past?

The hopes to bypass, the vast issues our relationship has amassed; was foolish, to say the least.

Is it realistic to dream of love without pain?

Do we sacrifice our happiness another day, month, and year?

Do we keep living a life with our hearts filled with tears?

Are we dimwits, that refuse to permit ourselves to commit;

The truth that somethings are required to end;

Dear God, I know you want me to be happy but how do I get there?

Dear God, I know you want me to be happy.

It's winter in my relationship cold icy temperatures, things seeming to be dead,

Hoping to awake from this nightmare; getting it's over through my fathead

The nutrients needed to reach the vessels are clogged.

The dream and reflection of a better time have been cataloged;

I understand today that everything must come to an end;

Foolish of me to wish for a better past

Wisdom has given me the peace to outlast

The poor decisions that led to this point and time

Where I internalize my choices, giving thanks for everything that happens in HIS DUE TIME!

PAY ATTENTION TO HIM

When a man puts you above all he loves and desires to keep you in the center of his life,

When that changes, he will make any change needed to restore it to its original state.

For him, failure is a pain as sharp as a knife. He lives with it daily giving it life.

When he stops sharing his thoughts and emotions with you there is a disconnection you have to solve.

For one reason or another, he doesn't feel safe sharing trusting you have become hard

Most men truly want peace in their homes over everything else.

That is his version of self-care; you must respect it and don't act like you don't care;

When a man doesn't desire to be intimate with you be careful of your rejection;

It's his way of showing affection; whether you agree with this or not

It will shape his future reactions; the worst thing that could happen is him losing his sexual attraction.

When a man lies he feels you can't respect or handle his truth

When a man cheats he has lost a level of respect for the relationship,

Himself or you.

Do you blame him for want to satisfy himself?

When you are not there for him in that way…why is it wrong for him to sway another way to satisfy his individual needs; should he suffer and do without because you want to play mind games; when there are countless opportunities to gain.

When a man doesn't care he will show you instead of telling you

When all of these are in your face, he has checked out of this relationship.

If you reflect on your past you will find what he tried to tell you.

Whether you listened, minimized his feelings or thoughts that up to you to decipher

But, from another man, I am here to tell you…we will ensure that part of us is satisfied.

I UNDERSTAND

I understand…I have to let things go

I understand…there are experiences that have to just flow

There are things we must go through to gain the wisdom

You said you wanted to leave, that you weren't in it anymore.

I felt it when we last made love knew it wasn't the same.

You said it's not the same anymore, that I look different.

The eyes have a way of showing you what is in your heart if you just listen

The pain, hurt, and turmoil has made our hearts so dark.

I understand things are never going to be the same a new life we must embark.

I understand we must create a new order to stay sane.

Where does love go? I wonder.

The understanding of the drift and disconnect is part of the growth away from each other.

When did we both make the decision to not investing in each other?

When did we decide we rather be with another?

The pain, hurt, and turmoil has made our hearts so dark.

I understand things are never going to be the same a new life we must embark.

I understand…I have to let things go

I understand…there are experiences that have to just flow

LIFE'S LESSONS

As I stare at the stars and reflect on life's decisions,

There were things I already knew;

There was a pain I had to endure and my mistakes only grew;

The path was dark, lonely and at times I lost who I was,

I hated who I'd become one without love

My emotions were flowing wildly it was so uncomfortable;

My mind filled with guilt, hurt, I was miserable

It reminds of how graceful a duck floats over the water from above;

We witness his grace from the top but not how much work his legs make to keep him afloat;

My heart and emotions are so out of alignment; I feel the darker inner thoughts controlling my every move; I put on my face and try to remain cool;

Destroying the house we built wasn't cool; Through it all, I had some fond memories that haunt me every day;

Things I could have done, moves I should have made, opportunities I missed; Life has a way of teaching you lessons & I've found that is the true blessing;

I'm stronger for it; the shit; was needed to make me better, took me to a depth I couldn't have imagined. The rebound or rise like a phoenix I could not have imagined

The headspace, my spirit is in a better place

I will continue to be open to the lessons, blessings, and opportunities with grace.

ABOUT THE AUTHOR

Demetrius Irick is a meditation coach, a social activist, Co-Founder of AkiliFlow, a Certified Professional & Executive Coaching Organization & Provoke Press, an independent self-publishing company designed to help first-time authors get their books published. Demetrius at his core believes his destiny is tied to helping individuals, couples, and organizations to reach their optimal performance using the Art of Meditation and Kemetic Yoga™□ as foundational principles and tools. Demetrius, a serial entrepreneur and best-selling author of "I'm Finally a Man, A husband's Journey to Manhood, has dedicated his life to the development of people and their God-given talents. Equipped with a pure passion to serve others, his mission is to help others begin the journey of becoming the best version of themselves reaching their spiritual, physical, and life goals.

OTHER BOOKS BY THE AUTHOR

- Meditation for Beginners: 8 weeks to a New life
- Live with Purpose
- I'm Finally a Man: A Husband's Journey to Manhood
- Ancient Wisdom
- Reflections in Time

www.ingramcontent.com/pod-product-compliance
Lightning Source LLC
Chambersburg PA
CBHW031604040426
42452CB00006B/400